WALKING IN KINDNESS

A Story of Compassion and Purpose through Setbacks and Comebacks

Denise Linton-Scott

Denise Linton-Scott
Lafayette, Louisiana
Website: https://walking-in-the-word.com

Limits of Liability and Disclaimer of Warranty
The author and publisher shall not be liable for your misuse of this material. This book is strictly for informational and educational purposes.

Warning – Disclaimer
The purpose of this book is to educate and entertain. The author and/or publisher do not guarantee that anyone following these techniques, suggestions, tips, ideas, or strategies will become successful. The author and/or publisher shall have neither liability nor responsibility to anyone with respect to any loss or damage caused, or alleged to be caused, directly or indirectly by the information contained in this book.

ebook ISBN: 979-8-9933581-0-9
Print ISBN: 979-8-9933581-1-6

Get Your Free Gift!

Pick up your free pdf journal to get started on Walking in the Word! I created it to assist you with applying God's Word to your life - whether it is to know who you are in Christ, get the answers to questions that you have, or with putting God's Word into practice. Plus, it is free!

It includes:

- Scriptures
- Prompts
- Affirmations

God to www.walking-in-the-word.com to receive your free gift.

Acknowledgments

My heartfelt gratitude to my loving husband, family, and friends who continue to support me and my dreams.

Donna Kozik, I am grateful for everything that you selflessly pour into me as my writing and publishing coach. Thank you, Elijah, for your time and assistance.

I would like to thank my coffee cooler and study hall community for your unconditional acceptance - you are my buddies who inspire and motivate me.

An extra special thank you to the individuals who have shown me kindness along the way.

Dedication

This book is dedicated to my husband, parents, brothers, family, friends, mentors, well-wishers, and you, my readers.

About the Author

Denise Linton-Scott is a leader, mentor, international speaker, and an author whose mission is to use her spiritual gift to encourage and inspire Christ followers to Walk in the Word, in addition to being hearers of God's Word. She does this in her "Walking In" Series where she writes about how she applies God's Word to her life and how others can do the same. Denise loves to connect with individuals and groups of women to share stories about how she is learning to walk in God's Word.

Denise worked in healthcare for more than three decades, and along the way she obtained her terminal degree - Doctor of Nursing Science (DNS) - in 2009. She was inducted as a Fellow of the American Association of Nurse Practitioners (FAANP) in 2020 for outstanding contributions and demonstrated commitment to advancing the nurse practitioner role. After careful consideration, she retired as a Professor in 2020 having taught nurse practitioner students for 11 years and being a certified and licensed Family Nurse Practitioner for 21 years. Now she is focused on her mission in which she incorporates lessons learned from a lifetime of passionately leading, serving, and encouraging others in various capacities.

Denise grew up in the hills of Rural Jamaica and immigrated to the US in 1990. She resides in Lafayette, Louisiana with her husband.

Get Denise's free PDF journal at
www.walking-in-the-word.com

Introduction

I am inspired by kindness. Throughout my life, I have been its recipient. God's gift to me is eternal life (Romans 6:23). Family, friends, and others give me their time, a home-cooked meal, or a gift. Their actions make me feel loved, happy, and like I belong. They put a smile on my face, a song in my heart, and a bounce in my steps. I even dance!

There are many people in our world who want to experience kindness. Some of them are alone, disadvantaged, or sick. And, the Holy Bible highlights widows and orphans (James 1:27).

These people are in our families, neighborhoods, at our workplaces, and in our churches. They may only need a smile, a hug, or a kind word.

This book is for you if you want to walk in God's Word and contribute to the health, and well being of others through kindness.

I am a retired Healthcare Provider, University Professor, and a 2020 Fellow of the American Association of Nurse Practitioners who has chosen to live a simple life. A life that allows me to take the time to strengthen my relationship with God. My pace is slower, I get to show kindness, and even grow what I eat. I embody self reflection, mindfulness, and intentionality.

I write books that encourage and inspire others to *Walk in the Word* in their relationship with God. My first book, *Walking in Trust,* tells the story of faith and resilience through trials. It is available on Amazon as a paperback and ebook at https://a.co/d/0p2jMWC. This second book is the answer to the question, *How can kindness help me do God's work?*

Contents

"Kindness first inspires kindness in others."

Unknown.

Chapter 1

Who Will She Become?

I grew up in rural Jamaica in the 1960s. My beginnings were humble and my parents had less than a high school education. But, they led an exemplary life, surrounded me with kindness, and ensured that my needs were met.

My late mother shared cooked meals and food supplies with people even if they did not express a need. She often covered a plate with food and asked me to take it to a neighbor. Other times, she gave me a bag with green bananas or other food to take to her best friend who lived a stone's throw away from us. She visited the sick and fed our family and friends in the small space that was our home.

I fell in love with food at a young age - *the way to my heart is through my stomach.* Mommy prepared scrumptious meals on the wood fire in our outside kitchen. My favorite breakfast was porridge - cornmeal, banana, or oats. I looked forward to our special Sunday dinners that consisted of Jamaican rice and peas, chicken, and a side of vegetables. The drink was usually a tasty cup of homemade juice from carrot or soursop - a tropical fruit that when ripe, is peeled, seeds removed, then the white pulp that remains is blended and sweetened to taste with a sweetener of choice, such as condensed milk. It was a change from the homemade lemonade that we drank during the week.

Daddy, who was a mechanic, was kind enough to repair vehicles free of cost for customers who could not afford to pay him. Oftentimes he allowed me to watch when repairs were done close to our home. I saw how to use a jack to lift a car up from the ground and how to change a tire. I saw him go to work outside the home from Monday through Saturday while Mommy worked at home.

I am the second child of my mommy. My parents taught my older brother, Howard and me to be kind to each other. He was a slender but strong light-skinned boy who was a bit tall for his age. His hair was always low cut and although he had a serious face, his smile lit up his face and revealed even white teeth. Howard willingly did the more difficult/complex chores and carried the heavier bags of groceries when we went to the corner store. He also climbed trees to pick fruits for our snack and cut sugar cane when I was too young to do so. He was responsible for me when we went anywhere together. He made me feel safe and I showed him respect (most times).

My world revolved around playtime, walking, and attending school without any complaint. I was a petite dark-skinned little girl with a cute round face, and beautiful smile. My thick blackish-brown hair, that was about shoulder length when braided, was admired by many. I walked to the home of family and friends to visit with them, take them food supplies from my parents, and play. Church and school - from pre-kindergarten to elementary school - were also within walking distance from our home. I still enjoy walking.

My first day of pre-kindergarten is one of my vivid early childhood memories. I was almost four years old. I was dressed in my uniform and had my double-sided slate with a wooden frame in hand. It comprised a small (approximately 8 by 11 inches) chalkboard with colored beads at the top.The beads assisted with learning colors and counting while I learned to write on the chalkboard section. I had to keep up with my older brother as we trotted to school, approximately fifteen minutes away. He is still a fast walker.

The other students were from our close-knit rural communities; we were between three to almost six years old. All of us sat in one large room on benches grouped together while our teacher, Mrs. Haughton stood at the front next to a blackboard. She often invited me to her home and to the church that she attended. My parents allowed me to go with her because she was an upstanding member of our community. This made me happy and it exposed me to the lifestyle of an educated person in the community.

Each evening after school, my aunt Norma (daddy's sister) who was our next door neighbor taught me to read. Aunt Norma was of average build, light-skinned with a smooth complexion, and short hair. I loved her contagious laughter then and even now. She taught me to read from the Nola book series that was popular in Jamaica at the time. We sat on the patio where I could see my older brother and neighbors at play. I whined and even cried to go join them but eventually gave in when she was not swayed. I soon began to look forward to our time together as it became our routine until I began elementary school at six years old.

Again, I accompanied my older brother, Howard, to school, this time it was elementary school. My first grade teacher, Miss Grant, was also my Sunday School teacher as well as the person who taught me at Vacation Bible School. She was tall, slim built with short hair, a pleasant face, quick smile, and a strong kind voice which she needed to teach a rambunctious group of first graders. She was a constant teacher in my life and I have fond memories of her happily giving me books as prizes for being able to memorize Scriptures accurately. I have wonderful memories of all my elementary school teachers. They were interested in what I had to say, praised me for being a well behaved student who excelled in classwork, and on those rare occasions disciplined me.

Jesus set the example of love and kindness to children when He allowed parents to take their children to Him. He held them, laid His hands on them, and blessed them (Mark 10:13, 14, 16).

The love of my parents and the kindness that I experienced from my family and community as a little girl gave me a strong sense of belonging and confidence. I felt safe and happy although I did not have modern conveniences such as electricity, indoor plumbing, or running water. Most of all, I saw grown ups who worked and showed kindness to their family and people in our communities. The seeds for me to do the same were planted.

SCRIPTURE

"Direct your children onto the right path, and when they are older, they will not leave it." (New Living Translation [NLT]).

PRAYER

Father God, thank you for my family and other communities that showed me kindness as a little girl.

Please equip me and use me to be kind to children who need to feel loved, safe, and like they belong.

In Jesus' name I pray.

Amen

REFLECTION

Make a list of your childhood influencers. Write about some acts of kindness that you received during your childhood.

"A little bit of kindness can change a life."

Unknown.

Chapter 2

The Unexpected

There was a horrible feeling in my stomach as I looked at the paper that told me where I placed in my class at the end of my first year in High School. Although I had failing grades on a few homework assignments and performed poorly on some examinations, I did not expect to be almost last in my class. *How could this be? I was usually first in my classes in elementary school. I even vied for first place in my class with two male friends and won most times. We were often first, second, and third.* My performance throughout the year was by no means stellar in any of my classes but I was still shocked, embarrassed, and I felt ill. I had determinedly worked hard and improved but apparently not quickly enough to make much difference. *Maybe I should be thankful that I did not place last.*

Since I did not want to feel that way ever again, I purposed in my heart to work harder, and believed that the result would be different in my second year.

I had decidedly chased away the negative thoughts and feelings about my setback and gone on to have an amazing summer. I excitedly began my second year in High School - *a new beginning*, I thought. My excitement waned after the first few weeks because my efforts were not yielding my desired outcomes. I was obtaining Cs and a few Ds on my assignments and examinations.

It was the weekend and I was sitting on the front porch of a deceased church member's home. It was customary in my rural community in Jamaica to gather at the deceased person's home for nine nights leading up to the funeral. People gathered in different places where they ate, reminisced about the deceased person, laughed, and played board games, including dominoes. The deceased daughter's fiancé, Reverend Fletcher, sat next to me and asked me how I was doing in school. I honestly informed him that I was almost last in my class during my first year. And, although I planned to do better during my second year I was already having challenges. I gave him an example of what I had difficulty grasping. I was learning about the parts of the hibiscus flower but I had difficulty remembering them. I vividly recall him asking me to fetch one and he and I identified and talked about each part as we separated it from the flower... sepals, petals, stamens (anthers and filaments), and the pistil (stigma, style, and ovary). To my surprise and delight I remembered the information during my examination!

Armed with this profound revelation of the type of learner that I am, I took the time to read and understand my textbooks and in class notes using practical application and association. I then made my own notes, created mnemonics, and reviewed them before each examination. It was very time consuming but I told myself that being a student was my job so I remained focused. What can I say, I was a serious young girl. I continued to improve and by the time I got to my third year, I was receiving academic awards. I was awarded the "Distinction in Caribbean History Prize" at the end of my final year.

As I reflect upon the kindness of Reverend Fletcher in the home of a deceased person, I am grateful that he took the time to ask a question that he wanted to know the answer to and that he was kind enough to assist me with something that was unrelated to us being at that place at that time. His act of kindness contributed to my success in high school and meeting the eligibility criteria to attend nursing school and be the first in my family to attend College.

I was reminded of Reverend Fletcher's kindness when a young girl needed me to assist her with algebra so that she could graduate from high school. I mentored her for months before her graduation from high school and throughout her undergraduate degree and PhD Program. I am happy that she allowed me to mentor her and pay forward what Reverend Fletcher did for me. I proudly refer to her as Dr. Mentee and I consider her my spiritual daughter.

Jesus was always kind to people when He was here on this earth. I think about when he fed more than 5000 people after He was told of the death of His cousin, John the Baptist (Matthew 14: 10-21). Jesus wanted to be alone to grieve His cousin but people sought after Him to heal those who were sick. As it got late, the people got hungry and Jesus' disciples suggested that they should be sent away to purchase food for themselves. However, Jesus said that they should be fed and when the disciples said they did not have enough to feed them Jesus asked for what they had. He blessed the five loaves and two fish that they brought to Him and was able to feed everyone, to their satisfaction. Opportunities for kindness present themselves in the most unexpected places and ways. Let us not miss them.

SCRIPTURE

"But the Holy Spirit produces this kind of fruit in our lives: love, joy, peace, patience, **kindness**, …" (Galatians 5:22, NLT).

PRAYER

Dear Lord, thank you for having a plan and a purpose for my life.

Please give me the strength to endure when I have setbacks in life.

In Jesus' name I pray.

Amen.

REFLECTION

Think about an unexpected act of kindness that you received when you were in dire need. Write a thank you letter to the person(s) who was/were kind to you - keep it or send it.

"We can't help everyone, but everyone can help someone."

Ronald Reagan.

Chapter 3

God's Promise - Hang On

It was the wee hours of the morning when my dad and I boarded a privately owned passenger vehicle that was bound for Kingston, Jamaica. We arrived at our destination more than four hours later as the sun was lighting the sky. I peeked through the window as the vehicle pulled up to the curb in front of the School of Nursing building. The sign at the entrance read, University Hospital of the West Indies School of Nursing.

I quietly exited the vehicle while my dad unloaded my light brown medium-sized suitcase and a few bags with miscellaneous items. He placed them next to me, quietly told me goodbye, returned to the vehicle, and they drove away.

I felt sad and alone as I thought, *This is where I will spend the next three years obtaining my Diploma in Nursing*. It was the first time that I would be that far away from home and I would not be returning home until our break - in a few months. My parents did not have a telephone so I would not be talking with them or my brothers.

There was a small welcoming committee - a faculty member had checked me in and a student nurse volunteer introduced herself to me - her name was Marcia and she was about to begin her second year. Marcia was slender with smooth even complexion, medium-length hair, and easy and quick smiles that showed her lovely dimples on her beautiful face. She accompanied me to the room that I was to occupy with a roommate during my first year - it was only about a five-minute walk away. We unpacked my modest belongings. Since I was the first student to arrive, I had an extended informal orientation time with her that I appreciated since it made me feel less sad and alone. It was also reassuring that she would be residing on the same ground floor a few doors away from me.

I woke up on the first day of classes with butterflies in my stomach. I donned my pink candy stripe uniform, combed my hair making sure that it was not on my collar, in accordance with the dress code, and placed my starched white cap on my head. I headed to the cafeteria for my breakfast - the cafeteria served us breakfast, lunch, and supper. I then returned to my room, grabbed my books, and went to the classroom in the School of Nursing building. Since I eventually had such a wonderful experience in high school I assumed that the same thing would happen here.

Alas, within a few weeks I was struggling to understand and retain the information that I was being taught. I made the decision to speak with a faculty member because she offered to assist my batchmates (classmates) and me. She spoke in a kind manner and besides that, her demeanor, age, and grey hair reminded me of my grandparents and the elderly ladies in my church home. She was a retired Matron (head of the hospital) who came out of retirement to teach us. I scheduled an appointment to speak with Matron Lambert and find out whether she had suggestions for me regarding how to be successful in my classes.

On the day of the appointment, I timidly knocked on her office door and entered when she responded. She asked me to have a seat when I entered. Matron Lambert wanted to know what she could do for me and she listened attentively as I spoke, not ever interrupting me. When I stopped talking, she asked me whether I read the Holy Bible and I replied in the affirmative and told her that I was a Christian. She proceeded to open her desk drawer and remove a well-worn Holy Bible which she opened to James 1:5, "If any of you lacks wisdom, you should ask God, who gives generously to all without finding fault, and it will be given to you" (New International Version, NIV). She told me that all I had to do was ask God for wisdom regarding all my classes and He would because His Word said so.

I had left my parents, brothers, and family, my church home, and what was familiar to me to obtain my first degree. The kindness of a volunteer student nurse allayed my initial feelings of sadness and loneliness about being far away from home for the first time in my life. She became my friend. During my three years in College, I had a wonderful community that was kind to me - from home-cooked meals to weekend visits to their homes, and adventurous day trips. This community included faculty, registered nurses in the hospital, batchmates, student nurses from other batches/cohorts, nurses residing in the nurses' residence, and my new church family members. I began attending a Church that was within walking distance from the nurses' residence and I became active in Sunday School and other church-related activities.

I had memorized scriptures in Sunday School, Vacation Bible School, and my personal devotion time but did not recall reading the scripture Matron Lambert shared with me: James 1:5, "If any of you lacks wisdom, you should ask God, who gives generously to all without finding fault, and it will be given to you." I truly believed those words and from that day I asked the Lord for wisdom so that I could be successful in the Nursing Program. Besides that, I resumed my studying strategies from High School. I went on to graduate and I am looking forward to celebrating my 40th-year reunion with my batchmates in 2026!

The kind faculty, Matron Lambert, taught me to apply God's word to my situation and I have not forgotten to do that. So, when confronted with anything difficult or unfamiliar, I speak James 1:5. I have shared this verse with my small group members, mentees, and many others along the way. Furthermore, I am learning to apply it to even things that are not difficult because I want to determine what God wants me to do instead of asking Him about my plans. Afterall, His Word says that He will instruct and teach us the way that we should go (Psalm 32:8).

SCRIPTURE

For I know the plans I have for you," says the LORD. "They are plans for good and not for disaster, to give you a future and a hope." (Jeremiah 29:11, NLT).

PRAYER

Father God, thank you for your faithfulness and for being a promise keeper of your Word.

Please give me the wisdom that I need to carry out this new project.

In Jesus' name, I pray.

Amen.

REFLECTION

Think about a time when you were far from family and friends and felt sad and alone. List the acts of kindness that you experienced and how they helped you.

"Twenty years from now you will be more disappointed by the things that you didn't do than by the ones you did do. So throw off the bowlines. Sail away from the safe harbor. Catch the trade winds in your sails. Explore. Dream. Discover"

H. Jackson Brown Jr.

Chapter 4

A Taste of Home

I lived and worked in Kingston, Jamaica since graduating from Nursing School in 1986 but I popped home unexpectedly quite often to see my family and enjoy home-cooked meals. I was at my parents home for two weeks before starting a new job. The day dawned, the day for me to leave my home again. This time it was beyond the shores of Jamaica to the United States (US).

My dad borrowed one of his friend's vehicles and he and Mommy accompanied me to the airport. We chatted along the way as Daddy left the hills and drove into the city to get us to the airport. We avoided the sadness - we would not see each other as often as we would like. This would be different from me being in Kingston approximately three hours away by car. We focused on how I was going to see my paternal grandmother, my aunt with whom she resided, my uncle-in-law, and my cousins.

Once again, Daddy removed my light brown medium-sized suitcase and bags with miscellaneous items from the vehicle. There were people everywhere, they talked, hugged, and shed a few tears as they said goodbye to their loved ones. I entered the airport and joined the long line to check in and drop my suitcase. It was to be my third time on an airplane but my first time to the US.

I immigrated to Brooklyn, New York in the US in February 1990 when I was recruited to work as a Registered Nurse (RN) due to the nursing shortage at that time. I thought that working in the US was an opportunity for me to be better able to satisfy my basic financial needs, assist my family members financially, and see my paternal grandmother, aunt and her family regularly. Besides that, I always wanted to visit the beautiful country of opportunities that I read about in books and saw in movies and television shows.

My nursing journey continued and I entered the job market in the PeriAnesthesia Care Unit (PACU) or Recovery Room (RR) in Brooklyn, New York with a bit of trepidation. The Operating Room (OR) was my preference because I had experience in that area and had completed a Certificate Course in Operating Room Techniques in Jamaica. However, there was no vacancy in the OR. I soon fell in love with the PACU because I was able to recover patients who had surgeries that were familiar to me. It was hard work but I believe that my training and experience in Jamaica prepared me, in addition to the hospital critical care course that I successfully completed, and my kind preceptor who was assigned to me for the first few months.

On this particular day, one of the Certified Nursing Assistants (CNAs) approached me. She was a tall beautiful lady with smooth dark skin, expressive eyes, and a quick smile. Miss Dee often engaged me in conversation and assisted me with my patients. Today she offered me some of her lunch and I graciously accepted. At the first bite I smiled delightfully as I tasted the love with which she prepared the meal - a very familiar emotional ingredient in all Mommy's meals - mixed in with the other ingredients. Her facial expression was one of relief and joy. That was the beginning of a wonderful relationship with my surrogate mother. She regularly brought me home-cooked meals made from scratch during the nine years that we worked together. Some of my favorite dishes were her chicken, lasagna, and roti. Her sweet potato and cornmeal pudding were divine.

I settled in to work and became proactive about my career. I began attending Medgar Evers College in Brooklyn to obtain my Bachelor of Science in Nursing (BSN) degree. I am a bit of a nerd so during my last semester, I decided that I wanted to be an advanced practice registered nurse who works in the outpatient setting instead of in the hospital. So, I enrolled in the Master of Science in Nursing (MSN) and Family Nurse Practitioner (FNP) Certificate Program at Columbia University

School of Nursing. Working full-time and attending school part-time left little time for me to prepare my meals but not to worry, my surrogate mother ensured that I was well fed.

I grew up in Jamaica surrounded by a community and the Lord blessed me in New York with a community. I had my extended family in addition to my work family, and later my church family at Brooklyn Tabernacle Church. I still missed my immediate family but I went back home to vacation at least twice per year.

I am happy that I was able to leave Jamaica to provide healthcare to patients in New York and further my nursing education and career. I was blessed by acts of kindness in the process. God's Word tells us that He is our shepherd and we will never want (Psalm 23:1). He provided for all my needs through people. For example, food through Miss Dee, like he provided manna (bread) from Heaven for the children of Israel as they journeyed to the Promised Land (John 6:31).

SCRIPTURE

"The people of the island were very kind to us. It was cold and rainy, so they built a fire on the shore to welcome us." (Acts 28:2).

PRAYER

Father God, thank you for always going ahead of me and preparing the place where I will be.

Thank you for the people that you bring into my life during my transitions. Please bless them and their family.

In Jesus' name.

Amen

REFLECTION

What are your takeaways from reading this chapter and how can you apply them to your life?

"Kindness is the language which the deaf can hear and the blind can see."

Mark Twain.

Chapter 5

Profession and Purpose

I have enjoyed taking care of people since I was a little girl. There were elderly persons in my community whom my mom allowed me to visit to help clean and organize their homes. My career goal was to work as a nurse in a hospital setting and care for sick people of all ages. When I became an RN it was not only about doing things that only the RN could do, such as medication, blood, and intravenous fluid administration. It was to do things that patients could not do for themselves.

I gave my patients mouth care, bed bath, clean bed linen, and assistance with meals - cut food into bite-sized pieces and reheat cold hot beverages or food. Besides that, when I worked in the OR in Jamaica I was sometimes assigned to assist the anesthesiologist. The patients were either scared of dying, that their surgery would not resolve their symptoms, or that they would have life-threatening complications. While in the preparation room (referred to as the anesthesia room at the time) separated from the operating room by a door, I reassured scared patients by telling them that I would be in the OR with them and held their hand while they were being put under anesthesia.

When I began working in PACU in the US, the patients complained of dry mouth because of the effects of the anesthetic agents and they often had nothing to eat from the night before surgery. However, they can not have anything to eat or drink until their bowel sounds are back. I kept their lips and mouth moist with a wet gauze and glycerine swabs. Some very thirsty patients were given water to swish and spit if they could be trusted not to swallow the water. Others were given ice chips if they had a physician's order for it. Privacy and dignity were maintained by ensuring that their gowns were the correct size and that they were covered properly with sheets and blankets as needed. Furthermore, dentures that had to be removed before going to the OR were put back or wigs that were askew were straightened as soon as possible.

My actions were different when I transitioned from the hospital to the outpatient setting as a Family Nurse Practitioner (FNP) in 1999. I was a primary care provider to vulnerable and underserved people many of whom had less than a high school education. I educated them about disease prevention and taught them how to promote their health and prevent worsening of their medical conditions in ways/terms that they could understand.

On this particular day, one of my patients was on a return visit to follow up her blood test results related to diabetes, high blood pressure, high cholesterol, and a possible autoimmune disease. She was wearing her usual wide smile that reached her eyes when she entered the room and we hugged. I sat across from her in the examination room. As she listened intently to the results and the lifestyle changes that she needed to make I was suddenly engulfed by a warm feeling. It rose up from the pit of my stomach and I immediately thought, *This is how Jesus felt when the Bible says that he looked at the crowd and had compassion on them and healed those who were sick* (Matthew 14:14).

My patients and I shared hundreds of hugs and I truly cared about them but a huge dose of compassion was deposited in me that day and I suddenly realized that what I had been doing in my profession was part of my purpose. Because I had more compassion for my patients, it was easy to be kind and patient with them. We worked together to get their numbers within the correct range, I came to understand their culture better, and was more creative with the lifestyle changes that I recommended.

After approximately five years, in 2004, I decided to obtain my Doctor of Nursing Science (DNS) Degree because I wanted to learn how to conduct research in the clinical setting and improve my patients' health outcomes. I attended Louisiana State University Health Sciences

Center (LSUHSC), School of Nursing in New Orleans, Louisiana. I began disseminating my research findings at local research conferences in 2007. In December 2008, I presented a poster at the LSUHSC, School of Nursing and Ochsner Clinic Foundation Fall Nursing Scholarship and Research Forum Scholar's Day in New Orleans, Louisiana. While I proudly stood next to my poster titled *Pap Smear Intention among Rural Southeast Louisiana Women,* I noticed a hot pink poster a few steps away. I curiously went closer and introduced myself to two people who said that they were faculty at an in-state university. We exchanged business cards. A few months later, I received an email from their Associate Dean who wanted me to call her. I received an invitation to join their faculty and found out that we were a good fit for each other after the interview process. So, I left my clinic job to work as an assistant professor at the University of Louisiana at Lafayette because there was a need for a family nurse practitioner with a doctorate in nursing. It was not in my plans to leave my full-time job with my patients but I believe that it was God's plan for me.

The compassion and kindness that I had for my patients extended to academia when I taught undergraduate nursing students from 2009 to 2010 and nurse practitioner students between 2009 and 2020. It warms my heart that I was able to prepare hundreds of nurses and nurse practitioners for the workforce in a kind and nurturing environment.

I thank the Holy Spirit for teaching me how to prioritize walking in kindness during my encounters with my patients and students. I am learning how to do the same thing within my family and communities. I hope that you either continue to do the same or begin to be more intentional about doing the same.

SCRIPTURE

"I knew you before I formed you in your mother's womb. Before you were born I set you apart..." (Jeremiah 1:5, NLT).

PRAYER

Thank you, Father, for all the people you placed along my path so that I could have a successful career and a purpose in life.

Please use me to pay it forward to others.

In Jesus' name.

Amen

REFLECTION

Think about where you are in your life right now. How did you get here and whom can you thank?

Get Your Free Gift!

Pick up your free pdf journal to get started on Walking in the Word! I created it to assist you with applying God's Word to your life - whether it is to know who you are in Christ, get the answers to questions that you have, or with putting God's Word into practice. Plus, it is free!

It includes:

- Scriptures
- Prompts
- Affirmations

God to www.walking-in-the-word.com to receive your free gift.

www.ingramcontent.com/pod-product-compliance
Lightning Source LLC
La Vergne TN
LVHW010942110826
845149LV00013B/2723
* 9 7 9 8 9 9 3 3 5 8 1 1 6 *